Irish Dancing Costume

Martha Robb

Series Editor: Michael Ryan

Country House, Dublin

Published in 1998 by
Town House and Country House
Trinity House
Charleston Rd
Ranelagh
Dublin 6

British Library in Publication Data: A catalogue record for this book is available from the British Library.

ISBN 0-946172-60-9

ACKNOWLEDGEMENTS

The author wishes to acknowledge the generous help she received from the many costume makers, dancers and dance teachers, too numerous to mention, who helped her in her research. Special thanks also to Mairéad Dunlevy, Keeper of the Art and Industrial Division, National Museum of Ireland, who commented on the manuscript.

The author and publishers would like to thank the following for permission to reproduce their photographs: Cora Cadwell (photo 6), Marion Carey (pls 8, 9, 14, 15), Mary Carey (photo 13 and pl 20), Peggy Carty O'Brien (photo 18), Cork Examiner (photos 7, 8, 10, 15, 16, 17), Cork Public Museum (photo 5), Dr John P Cullinane Archive Collection, Cork (photos 3, 9, 11, 14, 20, 22), Maureen Haley (pl 16), Chris Hill (pl 17), The Irish Times (pl 13), Tadhg Keady (pls 7, 11, 18, 19), Margaret McErlean (photo 19), Sylvia Murphy-Brennan (pl 6), Helen Parker (photo 21), Nora Redmond (photo 12), June Threlfall (pl 12), Traditional Music Archive (photo 1), Ulster Museum (photos 2, 4). The remaining photographs are by the author.

With the exception of photo 3 and 22, photographs from the Cullinane Archive Collection were originally published in *Irish Dancing Costumes* by JP Cullinane (Cork 1996).

Cover photo by Slide File, Dublin

Typeset by Typeform, Dublin

Printed in Ireland by βetaprint, Dublin.

CONTENTS

Photo 1: Mazie McCarthy, prize dancer, piper and drummer, Alice Dunne, prize dancer, May McCarthy, union piper, wearing brat *and* léine *style costumes and 'Tara' brooches (1906). Mazie McCarthy's costume features an early example of 'Kells' or Celtic-style embroidery. Originally published in* Irish Minstrels and Musicians, *by Francis O'Neil (Chicago, 1913), entitled 'Irish cailíní' (girls).*

IRISH NATIONAL DRESS

Irish dancing costume evolved from the desire to wear a distinctive national Irish dress, an idea that had some vogue at the turn of the twentieth century, under the influence of the Celtic Revival. Irish tradition and culture, including native Irish forms of dress, had been challenged by English rule in Ireland: as far back as 1536, Henry VIII attempted to ban indigenous Irish dress styles with a decree that 'no man or man child should wear no mantle in the streets but cloths or gowns shaped after the English fashion' (E F Sutton, *Weaving: The Irish Inheritance* (1980), p 14). During the Celtic Revival, nationalists in Ireland aspired to re-establish pride in native Irish traditions, as did their counterparts in Hungary, Finland and Norway, countries that were also seeking national independence. The wearing of distinctive Irish costume was encouraged as one manifestation of the growing spirit of national consciousness, though it never become an everyday garb for any but the most ardent nationalists.

The Gaelic League

The Gaelic League, founded in 1893 to stimulate renewed interest in the Irish language and culture, was an important element in the Celtic Revival movement. Douglas Hyde, a founder member, spoke of the need to 'de-anglicise the Irish nation'. Dress was seen as one way of doing this: Nellie O'Brien, an executive committee member of the Gaelic League, declared in 1911, 'the man who has the Irish language on his lips will wish also to have Irish clothes on his back' (*An Claidheamh Soluis,* 30 December 1911, p 7).

Promotion of Irish textiles

Textiles manufactured in Ireland at the turn of the century included woollen cloth, linen and poplin. Lace and embroidery were important craft industries. The Irish Industries Association was established in 1886 by Lady Aberdeen, wife of the Viceroy, to promote Irish industries and in particular the making of lace. The Congested Districts Board, a government agency established in 1891 to alleviate poverty, encouraged spinning, weaving, knitting, crochet and lace work in the most economically depressed, agricultural regions.

Photo 2: Dancing in the Glens, Co Antrim c. 1900. The dancers are wearing everyday clothes.

Photo 3: Group of dancers and musicians who toured America c. 1900. The dress of the female dancers is a fanciful 'stage' representation of Irish peasant dress of the nineteenth century, associated with the idealised image of the Irish 'colleen'. The skirts were short for the period, probably to allow for ease of movement in dancing.

John Cullinane Archive Collection

6

Photo 4: Cassie O'Neill wearing her everyday or Sunday best dress, which is probably of Irish manufacture, Glenarm Feis 1904. In that year, Evelyn Gleeson of the Dun Emer Guild judged the industrial section at the first Glens Feis, including competitions for the boy and girl best dressed in Irish materials made up in the Glens.

International, national, provincial and local exhibitions of Irish art and industry were significant in the promotion of Irish textiles of innovative design. Around the time of the Cork Industrial Exhibition of 1883, reform of Irish lace design, for example, was undertaken by James Brenan, the headmaster of the Cork School of Art, together with Alan Cole, a needlework expert from the South Kensington Museum in London. In 1901 the Gaelic League initiated a campaign to encourage Irish industries in the hope of decreasing emigration and in the belief that the revival of Irish pastimes and support for local industries would provide prosperity and employment. In 1907 Lady Aberdeen's Lace Ball advertised lace as a fashion fabric.

'Kells' embroidery

Alice Hart, who established the Donegal Industrial Fund in 1883, was responsible for the development of 'Kells' embroidery, inspired by a revival of Celtic ornamentation taken from the Book of Kells. This style of embroidery was carried out on handspun and vegetable-dyed linen, wool, or Galway flannel, using polished flax thread. 'Kells' embroidery was displayed for the first time at the Inventions Exhibition in London in 1885, where it was awarded a gold medal, and it became a feature of many Irish dancing costumes (see photo 1).

Style of national costume

While many of the urban middle classes were content to demonstrate their affiliations with the Revival movement by wearing fashionable tailored everyday clothing of Irish manufacture, ardent supporters of Gaelicism wanted to have a national costume for special occasions that demonstrated a more overt sense of Irish identity. A 1919 edition of *Leabhar na mBan* (a women's journal which followed the progress of Cumann na mBan, the women's section of the Irish Volunteers) advocated the wearing of Irish costumes:

> ... apart from the national idea expressed in the Gaelic costume, it is very practical and economical. The ideal thing is to have the dress and the brat of Irish material... [during the war]... it was almost impossible to get anything of Irish make except heavy tweeds, but we will hope that the manufacturers will soon give us our beautiful stuffs again. Poplin is always there for those who can afford it.

The Dun Emer Guild (named after Cú Chulainn's wife Emer, who was endowed with 'the gift of embroidery and all needlework') was a craft workshop adhering to a broadly based Arts-and-Crafts ideology. It was founded in 1902 by Evelyn Gleeson, a follower of the Gaelic League and supporter of the Arts-and-Crafts movement in Ireland, and the Yeats sisters. Girls at the guild were employed to make beautiful things in the spirit and tradition of the country. The guild used Celtic-style embroidery in its work.

The journal also included an advertisement for 'Embroidered Irish Costumes' made by the Dun Emer Guild.

Costumes were invented from knowledge gained from archaeological, philological and antiquarian research carried out from the early 1800s onwards. They were inspired by medieval dress and ancient Irish dress styles from the Early Christian period. One source was Eugene O'Curry's *Manners and Customs of the Ancient Irish* (Dublin, 1873). He concluded that the *léine* (a sleeveless, tunic-style linen garment, often of ankle length) was worn in early Christian Ireland by both men and women of the wealthy classes. It was slipped over the head

Photo 5a: The male dancer, who is here accompanied by Tomás MacCurtain on the violin, is wearing fall breeches, shirt and bow tie (Cork c. 1915). Fall breeches, which evolved in the early eighteenth century, had a 'fall' or flap, buttoned up to waist level, covering the central opening of the trousers.

Photo 5b: Detail of cummerbund; it appears to be embroidered with a harp motif.

and gathered at the waist using a belt. Shorter *léinte* (tunics), reaching to the calves, were worn by people involved in physical work or by the poor. A rectangular *brat* (cloak), also worn by men and women, falling to the ground from the shoulders, could be fastened with a brooch. It was made from wool and was usually colourful, sometimes having a fringe or decorative border of embroidery. Its length and quality was indicative of social class.

At the Gaelic League's *Oireachtas* (Irish cultural festival) exhibition of 1911, models of Irish national costume, made by the Dun Emer Guild and Cuala Industries, were displayed, and similar costumes were worn by many women attending the event, while some of the men wore kilts (favoured at

Photo 6: Cora Cadwell, winner of national costume competition, Tailteann Games, Dublin 1924. Her costume of green poplin with green, purple and gold embroidery was made by the Dun Emer Guild. The girdle was made in the same silk threads as the embroidery. Her socks were crocheted by the nuns of Beaumont and her shoes made by Whelans of Parnell Street, in Dublin. She later wore this dress for dancing.

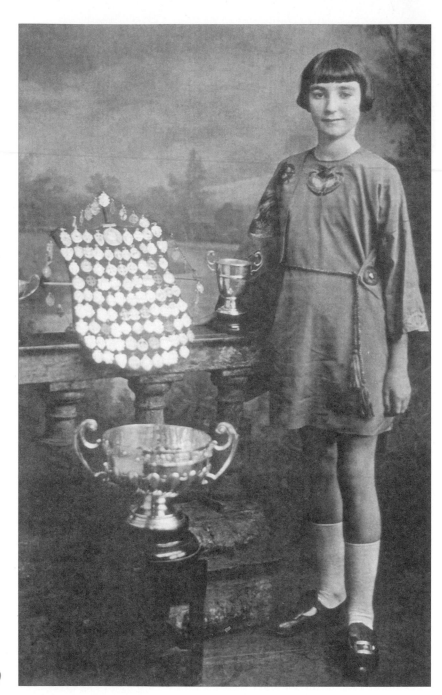

10

Photo 7: B Coleman, M Coleman, N Lawton, C Broderick, B O'Shea, N Tarrant, N Mahony, S Leahy, M Manning, E Finn, L Donovan, May Canty, C Mahony and James Barrett at the Father Mathew Feis (Cork 1928)

the time as a form of national dress for men). A 1912 report of the Wexford Feis in the *Catholic Bulletin* (a monthly journal first published in 1911) commented that convent schools had been involved 'in the making of beautiful national costumes, a delight to the judge'. Costumes similar in style to those made by the Dun Emer Guild were advertised in the nationalist newspaper *An Claidheamh Soluis* (1 March 1914, p 2, 8, 10 and 4 April 1914, p 8) as suitable Irish national costume. On 3 July 1915, the same paper reported that the Carlow Feis 'attracted hundreds of competitors… The dress competitions are a challenge to the tawdry imported fashions.' Costume competitions became a regular feature of *feiseanna* as supporters of Gaelicism, including Irish dancers, were encouraged to wear styles of dress which demonstrated affiliation with the nationalist cause.

11

REVIVAL OF IRISH DANCING

*At the Oireachtas of 1911 the programme included a pageant of 'A Feis at Tara' which was a fanciful reinvention of an ancient fertility festival. The term **feis** came to be used for a smaller, regional version of the Oireachtas.*

The Gaelic League played a leading role in encouraging Irish dancing, both in the form of the *céilí* or recreational, social dance and in the form of competitive dancing. It organised its first *céilí* in London, in 1897. Soon *céilithe* were being held in Dublin.

The first Oireachtas organised by the Gaelic League was held in Dublin, also in 1897. This was a cultural festival constituting a programme of Irish literature, music, song and dance. It became an annual event and, in later years, also featured art and industrial exhibitions. The first Gaelic League Industrial Exhibition took place at the annual Oireachtas in 1904.

The first modern *feis* was held in Macroom, County Cork, on 20 March 1898, and competitions for Irish dancing included those for best hornpipe, reel and jig. Provincial *feiseanna* were held for the first time in Belfast and Cork in 1900. Industrial exhibitions on a small scale were common at *feiseanna*.

Political events

A bill granting Home Rule (a limited form of independence) to Ireland was passed in 1914, but when World War I broke out, Home Rule was suspended until the end of the war. This made many Irish nationalists impatient. On Easter Monday, 1916, the Irish Republican Brotherhood rose up against British rule and proclaimed a republic. The leaders of the rising soon surrendered and were executed, but the rising was succeeded by the War of Independence (1919-20).

In 1921 the Anglo-Irish Treaty, creating the Irish Free State and the state of Northern Ireland, was negotiated. Not all nationalists were happy with the treaty, and a civil war ensued (1921-1922).

Dancing schools

The popularity of *feiseanna* led to increased demand for tuition in Irish dancing. The National School of Irish Dancing was opened in Dublin in 1913. Cormac Mac Fhionnlaoich was teaching dancing in Dublin in 1915. Lily Comerford opened a class for children in the early 1920s.

Photo 8: Bridie Coleman, John Whitley and Margaret Coleman, winners of the senior three-hand reel at the Father Mathew Feis (Cork 1930)

After the creation of the Irish Free State in 1922, enthusiasm for Irish dancing continued to grow. In the 1920s, as more dancing schools were established, Peggy Medlar had a school in Dublin, Essie Connolly conducted a school in her home near Pimlico, Jim Johnston founded a school in Belfast and Mrs Mulholland had one in Derry. Cormac Ó Caoimh taught in Cork and Joe Halpin in Limerick.

An Coimisiún le Rincí Gaelacha

An Coimisiún le Rincí Gaelacha (The Irish Dancing Commission) was established in 1929 in order to promote and preserve Irish dancing and to improve the organisation of dancing groups and competitive events. In 1931 the rules of An Coimisiún le Rincí Gaelacha were approved by the Gaelic League.

13

Photo 9: Tomás Ó Faircheallaigh, a founder member of An Coimisiún le Rincí Gaelacha, wearing the Ulster belt which he won in 1929 and 1931 with his sister Eileen (later McCormick), c. 1930.

John Cullinane Archive Collection

DEVELOPMENT OF DANCING COSTUME

With the revival of Irish dancing, the distinctively Irish costumes that were worn as an expression of nationalism were also worn for dancing.

Dancers had traditionally worn their everyday or Sunday best dress to dances (photo 2), but to express their national identity, women attending the Gaelic League's *céilithe* were encouraged to wear green skirts. In 1901 the Gaelic League directed that no prize be awarded to a competitor in an Oireachtas unless the competitor was dressed in clothes of Irish manufacture,

Photo 10: The capes and aprons worn by this group of competitors in the Father Mathew Feis of 1931 are reminiscent of stage presentations of nineteenth-century peasant dress, associated with the Irish colleen.

and the Gaelic League Industrial Committee, established in 1902, made a similar recommendation in March 1903 for competitors at all *feiseanna*.

Influence of rural dress styles

In 1913, the fashion columnist in *An Claidheamh Soluis* expressed the wish to preserve the dress of the 'Gaeltacht, the costumes of the Claddagh women, the Aran Islanders and the Kerry *cailíní*. Costumes worn by many dancers (including Maighdlín Breathnach and Eibhlín Nic Fhionnlaoich featured in *An Claidheamh Soluis* on 28 February 1914, p 12, and by dancers in the Cork Pipers' Club in 1915) featured hooded cloaks. Traditionally, hooded cloaks had been worn in all parts of Ireland and over much of Europe during the nineteenth century. The late Cormac O'Keefe commented that girls from the Jim Johnston School in Belfast, clad in white dresses and green hooded cloaks and competing in dancing competitions at the 1924 Tailteann Games, were wearing the proper traditional costume (J P Cullinane, *Aspects of the History of Irish Dancing* 1994, p 64).

Other elements of rural or peasant style dress also influenced the style of Irish dancing costume worn at *feiseanna* (see photos 10 and 16). The application of bands of braid to the hemlines of *báinín* (homespun woven

15

Two 'Irish villages' were constructed at the Columbian Exposition in Chicago in 1893, showing a romantic and picturesque portrayal of Irish village scenes, including Irish colleens in peasant dress demonstrating textile crafts, household chores and Irish dancing. Similar village scenes were established at Olympia in London in 1888, in St Louis in 1904 and at the Imperial International Exhibition in London in 1909. Although these visual effects were successful in marketing Irish products, they were felt by some to be patronising and to reinforce stereotypes of Ireland as a backward peasant society.

woollen cloth) dresses dyed red, worn by dancers in Galway from the 1950s to the 1970s (as illustrated in *My Irish Dance*, by Peggy Carty O'Brien), was reminiscent of the Connemara petticoat, traditionally worn in the area during the nineteenth century and up to the middle of the twentieth century (see also photo 3).

Peasant dress of the nineteenth century, which has 'much claim to be an Irish national costume' (Timothy O'Neill, *Life and Tradition in Rural Ireland*, (1977), pp 44-5), had some influence on the development of Irish dancing costume, but not as much as might have been expected. That may have been because nationalists did not want to be associated with a style of dress that was too 'stage Irish'. It is also apparent that middle-class Gaelic Leaguers did not favour the wearing of a costume associated with a peasant society. In any event, the hooded cloak was recognised as being too cumbersome for dancing and went into decline in the 1920s.

Class and solo costumes

By 1930 the wearing of a *class costume* was an established practice. A class costume is worn by a dancing school group. Combination of style, colour and decoration used in the design allows the costume to carry the identity of the particular school.

In addition to class costumes, most female dancers have *solo costumes*, to wear when they perform solo. These costumes became increasingly popular in the late 1970s and are the most elaborate Irish dancing costumes. The solo costume is dictated by the dancer's own personal colour preference, choice of design and embroidery motifs.

Dress design

Costumes derived from the *brat* and *léine* were worn by many Irish dancers from the turn of the twentieth century. For example, costumes of this type, worn in dancing competitions at the Mater Carnival Dublin, were illustrated in the *Irish Independent* of 27 September 1922. Girls competing in dancing competitions at the Tailteann Games, in celebration of the new Free State and held in 1924, 1928 and 1932, wore similar costumes.

Costumes worn for Irish dancing continued to draw inspiration from authentic or imagined ancient dress styles, rural peasant dress and fashionable

cont. p 20

*Pl 1a and b:
Solo costume in
gabardine, featuring
inverted pleat and
the initials of the
dancer (Anne
McErlean of the De
Glin School of Irish
Dancing, Derry (An
Coimisiún)) on the
skirt front,
embroidered by
Máire Stafford in
Galway (1975).
A gold-coloured lace
collar and brown
velvet bodice
complete the outfit.*

17

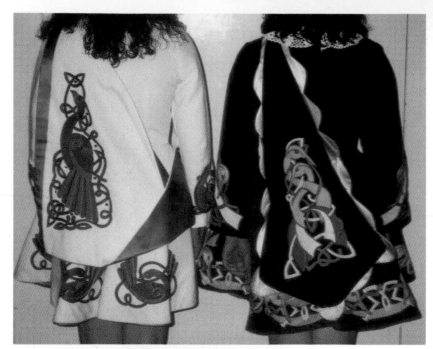

Pl 2 (above): Solo costume in Trevira with turn-back triangular brat, *worn by Patricia McLean and solo costume in velvet with kite-shaped* brat *featuring scalloped edge, worn by Lisa McLean, both of the Gillan School of Irish Dance, Dunloy, Co Antrim (An Coimisiún) (1994). Both costumes are hand-embroidered.*

Pl 3 (left): Solo costume in black velvet, featuring an inverted pleat with green satin lining, mandarin-style collar and rhinestones, worn by Shauna Gillan of the Gillan School (1994) and made by Ellen Doherty, Ringsend, Co Derry.

18

Pl 4 (right): Solo costume made in Trevira by Ellen Doherty (1990), featuring a box pleat and chain-stitch hand embroidery by Threads of Green, Kilkenny. Glass rhinestones decorate the dress.

Pl 5 a and b (Below left and right): Black velvet solo costume, worn by Claire McCamphill, Gillan School (1994) and made by Margaret Devlin, Ballinderry, Co Derry. It features an inverted pleat lined with contrasting fabric of metallic gold lamé, kite-shaped brat with scalloped edge and turn-back embroidered cuffs, and an Irish crochet lace collar. Transfer designs from Seven Gates Designs, Drogheda. Machine satin stitch embroidery and appliqué by Threads of Green, Kilkenny.

19

Pl 6: Orla Brennan of Murphy-Brennan Irish Dance Academy, Birmingham (An Coimisiún) (1992/3) wearing a solo costume made by Christine Angliss of England. Appliqué is used as well as embroidery to create the Claddagh design, and the collar is hand-crocheted.

cont. from p 16

dress. Competitions for best Irish costume continued to be held at *feiseanna*, including a class for the prettiest Gaelic costume at the Ballymena Feis of 1931. A special prize was awarded to the dancing competitor most suitably dressed in Irish costume at the Nenagh Agricultural Show on August 18th 1937.

In some areas of Ireland, girls wore kilts for Irish dancing until the late 1940s (photos 8, 11). The kilt was most often worn with a blouse, bolero jacket and brat. Pleated knee-length dresses were popular as class costumes well into the 1950s and were still worn by some dancers in the 1980s (photos 9, 12–16, 18–20). These dresses were probably inspired by a combination of the kilt, a fashion for pleats and possibly evidence that a style of dress with folded pleats had been worn in Ireland in the sixteenth century (provided by John Derricke's *Image of Ireland*, 1581). By the 1950s, however, dresses with a circular style of skirt were popular (photos 21–2).

20

cont. p 23

Pl 7: Members of the Murphy-Brennan Irish Dance Academy at the World Championships (1997) wearing costumes by Christine Angliss and matching hair accesories. Appliqué is used as well as machine embroidery to create the bird designs on the dresses.

*Pl 8 a and b, Pl 9:
These costumes worn
by Sinéad Mullane
(pl 8) and Melissa
Keane (pl 9) at the
Munster
Championships
(1997), featuring
musical instruments
and dancing shoes,
suggest a move
beyond traditional
Celtic themes.*

22

cont. from p 20

Dancing organisations and costume style

The rules of An Coimisiún le Rincí Gaelacha (established in 1931) directed that dancers entering competitions contrary to its rules would be unable to compete at its *feiseanna*. Before this, the British Federation of Music Festivals programme included dancing competitions. Now dancers who continued to enter these festivals in the north of Ireland were unable to compete in *feiseanna*. The result was a split in the organisation of Irish dancing.

In 1972 the Festival Dance Teachers' Association was formed in the north of Ireland. It organises four festivals and an Ulster championship annually. Until the late 1970s, the styles of dresses worn by Coimisiún and Festival dancers were similar, the circular style of dress skirt remaining popular with female dancers (photo 22). However, Festival dancers tend not to have solo costumes and to wear class costume for solo dancing.

The rapid development of An Coimisiún le Rincí Gaelacha class and solo costumes in the last two decades can be attributed to the more competitive level of Coimisiún dancing. Coimisiún dancers enter local, provincial, national, and international *feiseanna*. Stiff competition motivates dancers to seek costumes which are innovative and individualistic in style and likely to be eye-catching during performance.

A dispute within An Coimisiún le Rincí Gaelacha in 1968 led to the foundation of a breakaway group called An Comhdháil Múinteoirí na Rincí Gaelacha (Confederation of Irish Dancing Teachers), which has groups throughout Ireland. The design of costumes worn by Comhdháil dancers developed along the same lines as those worn by Coimisiún dancers (pl 14).

During the 1980s an inverted pleat was a popular feature of Coimisiún costumes (pls 1, 3). Another development was the adoption of the box pleat, sometimes referred to as the 'apron front' (pl 4). Often the pleats are insertions of fabric in contrasting colour. During the dance, these inserts become visible adding to the dramatic impact of the dress.

23

Pl 10 a and b: Leisa McIntyre and Julie O'Connell of Loughguile Dancing Club, Co Antrim (Festival) (1994) wearing class costume in white Trevira and red satin featuring inverted pleats, cape-shaped brats *and hand-embroidered shamrock motifs. Lace collars are in traditional rose and shamrock pattern.*

FEATURES OF IRISH DANCING COSTUME

Fabric and colour

Costumes worn at the turn of the century were made from wool, *báinín*, linen and poplin. Favoured colours were green, saffron or white.

With the invention of synthetic fabrics starting in the 1940s, the woollen, linen and poplin industries went into decline. Trevira, made from polyester fibre (invented in 1967), and gabardine are currently popular, and Viyella, polyester twill, Lirelle and Terylene have all been used in making Irish dancing costumes. Velvet of synthetic fibre is very fashionable just now, particularly for solo costumes (pls 2, 3, 5).

Contemporary costumes appear in many colours, including black, purple, red, blue, green and white. Panelling, using fabric of different colours to

Pl 10 a and b (cont.):
The shamrocks on the dresses
and brats *derive from shamrock*
sprig designs. Sprigging
(decorating linen or muslin with
white hand-embroidery) was
popular as a home industry in
the late nineteenth and early
twentieth centuries.

make up a garment, is increasingly popular. Costumes are usually lined with satin of a contrasting colour. Pelmet stiffening, which has been used in costumes for over 10 years, makes the dress sit out, displaying the panels of embroidery.

Brat design

The *brat* is often referred to as a shawl. Rectangular or square *brats* popular during the 1920s, 1930s and 1940s were draped over both shoulders and secured at each side with 'Tara' brooches (photo 18). Alternatively, two corners were pinned together on the front of the dress at waist level (photo 9). Over the years a cape version attached to the dress at both shoulders became popular (photo 14, 21, pl 10). *Brats* fastened at one shoulder with a 'Tara' brooch and secured at the waist on the opposite side at the back were another common variation (photos 1, 8, 15, 19, 22, pl 1).

25

cont. p 28

Pl 11: Darran McHale of the Doherty School, Coventry (An Coimisiún), at the World Irish Dancing Championships (1997) wearing trousers and shirt. By contrast, Christopher Doyle of the Armstrong School, Belfast (An Coimisiún), is wearing a kilt, jacket and brat.

Pl 13 (opposite): Richie Reece of the De Burca School, Ohio, competing in the World Irish Dancing Championships (1994)

Pl 12: Black velvet cummerbund with gold lamé, orange nylon satin appliqué and fluorescent polyester thread work, worn by Joseph Threlfall of England with a shirt and trousers (1998)

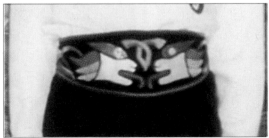

26

cont. from p 25

Pl 14: Bronagh Doherty wearing the class costume of the Coyle School of Irish Dancing, Inishowen, Co Donegal (An Comhdháil) (1994). Made in Trevira by Bridie Doherty of Clonmany and hand-embroidered by the dancer's mother, Janet Doherty (née Coyle).

Pl 15: The main motif on this heavily embroidered and appliquéd costume, worn by Gemma Donovan at the Munster Championships (1997), is the Salmon of Knowledge.

Two of the most popular forms of *brat* worn by contemporary female dancers are those of the turn-back triangular variety and the kite-shaped *brat* (pls 2, 5). Sometimes these are embellished with a scalloped edge. The size of *brat* has been decreased to facilitate vigorous movements in dancing, thus tending to become a neater and smaller accessory garment.

Motifs

Motifs on female costumes worn during the 1920s and 30s were often of a simple Celtic interlace design covering a small area of the bodice and *brat* (photos 6, 9, 12–14). Motifs sometimes featured harps or shamrocks. By the 1950s, the inclusion of embroidered motifs on the skirt was common (photo 21). Sometimes the initials or name of the dancing school featured in the decoration of the dress (photos 15, 16, 19). Shamrocks, though sometimes considered 'stage Irish', are still popular with some dancers.

28   Original designs for embroidery can be drawn directly on to costumes, or

Pl: 16: Tara Lavelle, Bethany Gould, Erin Blake and Andrea Drummond of the Haley School of Irish Dancing, Whitman, Massachusetts (An Coimisiún), wearing solo costumes (1997) made by Threads of Green, Kilkenny and Thomond Dancewear, Limerick

heat transfers can be used. Seven Gates Designs of Drogheda (established in 1988) produces an annual catalogue of heat transfer designs. Transfer designs are also available from Deighton's, England. The Book of Kells continues to inspire many Celtic and zoomorphic motifs. Designs are often much freer than the drawings in the manuscript, however, some using loose loops instead of interlace. Hounds, snakes, Irish harps, the 'Tara' brooch, the Claddagh ring, torc neck pieces, Celtic monograms, family, county, city and provincial coats of arms and round towers are amongst the motifs used (see for example pls 1 and 6). A good design for a dancing costume is triangular, with the apex at the waist. Birds are a popular form of decoration, providing scope for colour (pls 2–5, 7).

At the World Championships of 1996, Seven Gates Designs launched a new range of designs based on the legends of the Salmon of Knowledge (pl 15), the Death of Brian Ború, Setanta and the Hound of Culann and the Legend of Gráinne and Diarmuid.

29

Pl 17: Riverdance Troupe with Jean Butler and Colin Dunne

Pl 18: Darinagh White of the Clifford-Crosbie Academy, London (An Coimisiún), at the World Championships (1997). Her plum-coloured velvet dress lined in shot silk, with beaded lace sleeves and lace trim at the waist decorated with beading, sequins and diamanté, was clearly influenced by Riverdance. It was designed and made by her mother, Emer White (née O'Dowd).
Pl 19: Julie Gillan of the O'Donoghue School, Co Meath (An Coimisiún), at the World Championships (1997). Her dress in black velvet and gold chenille with machine embroidery was designed by An Siopa Rince in Dublin. The trend towards shorter dresses that followed Riverdance has been modified by a recent rule of An Coimisiún.

Embroidery and appliqué

At the beginning of the century, hand-embroidered chain stitch or, less frequently, satin stitch were used to decorate costumes, and embroidery was usually done in the dancer's home. Nowadays embroidery is more often carried out by dancewear companies and over the last fifteen years, dressmakers and dancewear companies are using an increasing amount of machine embroidery and appliqué. Decoration now covers a much greater area of the costume (pls 3, 5, 16, for example). Synthetic threads used in machine satin-stitch embroidery include rayon, neon polyester and lamé. Colours of nationalism are still common in embroidery (pl 3), though a freer use of colour is more evident.

31

Pl 20a: Brigid Kelly, wearing the class costume of the Johnston School, Belfast (1930s).

Pl 20b: Detail of the All-Ireland Championship belt won by Brigid Kelly, c. 1936.

Appliqué is carried out (pls 5b, 6) using for example satins, acetate satins, velvet or metallic lamé. Additional embellishment of rhinestones and diamanté stripping are options (pls 3, 4).

The average price of a class costume today is £350. Solo dresses, however, if heavily embroidered and with diamanté and unique features, can cost £800 or more.

Collars and cuffs

Lace collars and cuffs have traditionally been worn in white but can be of any colour (photos 11, 22, pls 1, 5 and others). In recent years the mandarin collar has become popular (pl 3) and embroidered cuffs are common (pls 1–3, 5).

Belt and socks

The belt has formed an important part of many costumes worn throughout this century (photos 1, 6, 14, 15, 19, 20). Today, it appears to be more commonly worn by Festival dancers (pl 10). White poodle socks (a style of ankle socks) are commonly worn. Black tights are also favoured, but more often for figure or group dancing.

Headgear

In the early part of this century some female dancers wore cloth head bands decorated with Celtic embroidery (photo 14). Sometimes berets or tam o'shanters with feathers were worn. Today, dancers competing at *feiseanna* favour a multicoloured range of hairbands and tiaras.

Shoes

Traditionally everyday shoes were worn by both male and female dancers. By 1924 light ballet pumps were being worn by female dancers performing the reel and slip jig at the Tailteann Games. Today these dances are performed by female dancers wearing cross-laced pumps, while male dancers generally wear lightweight shoes.

Hitherto it was mainly men who performed heavy jigs and hornpipes, and they wore their everyday shoes. However, around 1930 women in all parts of Ireland took to wearing heavy shoes with toe pieces in order to perform these dances. Nail toepieces can be added to both male and female dancing shoes to bring out the beats when battering. Alternatively, contemporary fibreglass toe pieces are used. Shoes are often decorated with buckles.

Medals

The practice of wearing medals to adorn costumes for festive and exhibition occasions began at the turn of the century. Medals won were attached to sashes or bodice fronts and, in the case of male dancers, to their cummerbunds or kilts, demonstrating success in competition (photos 1, 7, 8, 12, 13, 18, 20). This practice was subject to ridicule by comedians, however, and is uncommon today. Perhaps with the increase in competitions, a dancer might be unable to wear all his or her medals anyway.

Photo 11: The introduction of white lace collars and cuffs on costumes is attributed to Lily Comerford, whose dancers are here wearing class costume (1932). Irish crochet lace was to become part of many Irish dancing costumes. Lily Comerford was also instrumental in the promotion of kilts as class costume.

John Cullinane Archive Collection

MALE COSTUME

Early costume

Long-tailed coats based on the formal dress styles worn at Dublin Castle during the eighteenth and nineteenth centuries were sometimes worn by men over their shirts for dancing. In later years, the coats were only worn for formal occasions such as posing for photographs. According to the fashion of the period, cravats (photo 3), jabots, bow ties (photo 5) and ties (photos 9, 11, 15, 17, 18, 20) have been worn for Irish dancing. Green or black waistbands were worn and sometimes these incorporated embroidery (photos 5, 17).

Knee-breeches

Trousers were commonly worn by men for Irish dancing, but according to a report in *The Gael* (Gaelic League monthly journal published in New York) in September 1903 (p 314) an effort was made by Captain Otway Cuffe, Sheestown, Kilkenny, an ardent supporter of the Gaelic movement, to introduce knee-breeches, stockings and brogues as a national costume for men. Knee-breeches, commonly worn by boys at this time, were worn by many Irish dancers until the late 1930s and early 1940s (photos 5, 8, 11, 17). However, *Punch* magazine and comic postcards regularly caricatured 'Paddy' wearing knee-breeches. The Gaelic League was not keen to encourage the wearing of a form of dress in which the Irish had been caricatured, and the wearing of knee-breeches for Irish dancing gradually died out.

Kilts

In 1901, responding to a request for his opinion on suitable garb for wear at nationalist functions, Padraic Pearse was influential in having the kilt adopted as a national costume for men. The notion that the kilt was authentically Irish was popularised in Eugene O'Curry's *Manners and Customs of the Ancient Irish*, (1860) and by P W Joyce in his *Social History of Ancient Ireland* (1903). However, H F McClintock, author of *Old Irish and Highland Dress* (1943), provides strong evidence that the kilt had never been worn in Ireland.

35

cont. p. 38

Photo 12 (top left): Nora Kelly, later Redmond, of Shanballey in Co Mayo, wearing medals won at local feiseanna (1934). Her dress was saffron and her brat dark green with embroidery of mauve, green, white, blue and yellow; both were made from Foxford wool.

36

Photo 13: Mary Kelly, later Carey, Johnston School, Belfast (1938). The finely pleated green Foxford serge class costume, lined with saffron, was made by the dancer's mother and included a harp motif in the centre of the brat and Celtic style embroidery. She is also wearing a gold-coloured girdle and two 'Tara' brooches.

Photo 14 : Mona Kinsella, a pupil of Essie Connolly, Dublin, wearing a green costume and three Tailteann Games medallions (c. 1935)

Photo 15: P Finn, P Cronin, E Varian and J Lehane, winners of the four-hand reel at Feis Riverstown (1946). The embroidered, circular badges indicate membership of the Hasson School of Dancing, Cork.

Some Irish dancers wore kilts very early this century, and their wear for dancing became more widespread in the 1920s. Kilts were commonly of saffron (a colour outlawed in Ireland by Henry VIII) or green and were worn with black or tweed jackets, white shirts, *brat*s, wool stockings and a black tie. By the mid-1940s many male dancers were wearing kilts teamed with jacket, shirt, tie, knee-socks and *brat*. This became the usual outfit for boys competing at *feiseanna* (photos 15, 18, 20, pls 11, 13).

Contemporary male costume

Kilts worn by boys today are made from wool, tweed or polyester gabardine. White, cream, saffron and green are popular (pls 12, 13). Usually the *brat*, similar in style to that worn at the turn of the century, is made in the same fabric and has a fringed edge. A crest is sometimes machine embroidered on the *brat*. In addition to the purchase price of the fabric, the cost of making up a kilt and *brat* is about £60.

Jackets in velvet have been popular for the last ten years (pls 11, 13). Jackets are also made in tweed and can be of contrasting colour. They range in price from about £120 to £200.

COSTUME DEVELOPMENT IN THE DIASPORA

From long before the Great Famine, men and women emigrated from Ireland, taking their Irish culture with them.

Dance and costume in the US

Art and industrial exhibitions at the turn of the century in Chicago, New York, St Louis and Boston, some organised by the Gaelic League, increased American interest in Irish national costume.

The champion dancers of the San Francisco Dancing Club are pictured in *The Gael* of October 1904. While the male dancers are wearing knee-breeches and tail coats, the female dancers are attired in 'colleen' style dresses. Publications entitled *National Dances of Ireland* by Elizabeth Burchenal (New York, 1924) and *The Dance, its Place in Art and Life* by T Kinney and M W Kinney (London,1914), which included photographs, further popularised suitable styles of costume for dancing. In 1912 *feiseanna* organised by the Gaelic League were held for the first time in New York, Boston, Chicago and Philadelphia. Plates 13 and 16 show contemporary costumes worn by American dancers.

Dance and costume in Australia

In Melbourne, as early as 1932, the Irish National Dancing and National Dress Promoters Association legislated for costumes. Rule 18, 'Dress for Girls', read as follows:

White blouse, green shawl (similar to piper's), green kilts (to reach at least 2 inches below the knee), green cap (piper's pattern), green stockings with green, white and gold tops, black shoes with buckles

A cape was sometimes worn instead of a shawl.

The regulations laid down for boys' costumes were:

Green shirt, green tie, green knee breeches, green stockings with green, white and gold tops, green sash with gold edging (ribbon type) and no head-dress.

In South Australia, in 1936, a costume rule stated 'no costume which can be interpreted as a caricature of Irish costume is permitted to be worn in dancing competitions'.

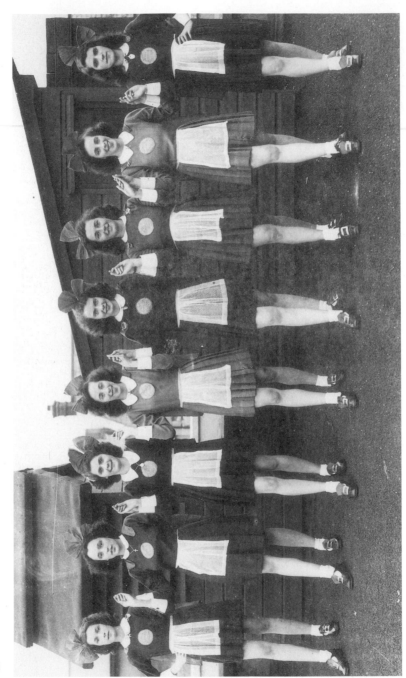

Photo 16: E McCarthy, K Rice, M Lehane, E McCarthy, L Dorgan, E Lehane, N Lehane, Hasson School, Cork, Munster figure dancing champions and winners at Kanturk Feis (1948). Hairbows reflect the fashions of the period and the white aprons are reminiscent of fanciful stage presentations of nineteenth-century rural peasant dress associated with the Irish colleen.

Photo 17: The outfits worn by these two boys at the Father Mathew Feis (1948) include short trousers and cummerbunds featuring a small amount of embroidery.

Dance and costume in Britain

Costume design was also evolving in Britain (photo 21, pls 12, 18). The London branch of the Gaelic League did immense pioneering work in promoting Irish dancing in Britain. The London Feis was inaugurated in 1907 and is still an event today.

World Championships

The World Irish Dancing Championships — *Oireachtas Rince na Cruinne* — has been an annual event in Ireland since 1969. Dancers from Britain, Ireland, America, Canada, Australia and New Zealand all compete. Affluence, ease of travel to and from competitive events and increased contact with other dancers have promoted worldwide similarity in costumes. Many overseas dancers prefer to obtain costumes in Ireland, and about half of the costumes manufactured in Ireland are exported.

Photo 18: Scoil Éilís Ní Shim, Galway (1949). Peggy Carty, later Carty O'Brien, is wearing a costume of cream viyella. The skirt is pleated all around and the Celtic embroidery is in red, green, purple and gold. 'Tara' brooches secure the brat. *Her brother, Val Carty, is wearing a green woollen kilt, a black collarless dress jacket with epaulettes and button trim and a square embroidered* brat.

Riverdance

Riverdance — performed for the first time on the occasion of the Eurovision Song Contest in Dublin in 1994 and subsequently an internationally popular show — offered a spectacular and innovative presentation of Ireland's traditional dance to a world audience (pl 17). Other shows, including *Lord of the Dance*, continued the trend.

A very different, modern style of dress was adopted for these shows. Though most female dancers still wear the more elaborate style of costume, the *Riverdance* outfits have had considerable impact, making new concepts of costume design possible for dancers (pls 11, 18, 19). Dresses in the new idiom are lighter than traditional costumes, facilitating ease of movement. Popular fabrics include velvet and chiffon. If embroidery is used, less complicated motifs decorate much smaller areas of the dress. Being simpler in design, these costumes are less expensive to buy.

The new fashion popular for male dancers consists of long trousers instead of kilts, with stylish shirts worn with or without a tie and sometimes with a cummerbund (pl 12) and/or a jacket or waistcoat.

As the twenty-first century approaches, *Riverdance* costumes seem set to continue to influence current trends in costume style. Whatever direction future fashion of male and female Irish dancing costume takes, it will reflect a self-confident modern Ireland, rich in traditions of music and dance, an Ireland which continues to reinvent its own heritage and to express its own national pride and identity.

Photo 19: The dancer on the left is Margaret McAlister, later McErlean, member of the Bridie Shiels School of Dancing, Ballymoney, Co Antrim (1951). Her costume was of light blue linen and worn with a yellow belt. The initials of the school are embroidered in gold on the bodice.

43

Photo 20: Ciss and
John Cullinane,
pupils of Tommy
Cullen. John is
wearing the belt
which he won at Feis
Mathew (1952,
1953, 1954),
previously competed
for as the All-Ireland
Championship belt.

44

Photo 21: Helen Parker, Ted Kavanagh School, London wearing class costume (1957). The green dress has a circular skirt and the costume is lined with gold satin. Embroidery is in mauve, blue, black, yellow and red. The brat *is fastened at the shoulders with two 'Tara' brooches.*

Photo 22: Members of Scoil Uí Chuilleanáin, Cork (1970). The women's circular skirts are of emerald green woollen material and the men's kilts are saffron, worn with tweed jackets and brats or shawls. John Cullinane Archive Collection

SELECT BIBLIOGRAPHY

Ajello, E, *The Solo Irish Jig*, London: C W Beaumont, 1932

An Claidheamh Soluis, 25 October 1913, p 8, 28 February 1914, p 12, 21 March 1914, p 2, 8, 10, 4 April 1914, p 8 , and 3 July 1915, p 4

Ballard, LM, 'Aspects of the History and Development of Irish Dance Costume', *Ulster Folklife*, 1994, vol 40, pp 62–7

Burchenal, E, *National Dances of Ireland*, New York: G Shirmer Inc, 1925

Carty, P, *My Irish Dance*, Galway: Connaught Tribune Ltd, 1987

Cullinane, J P, *Aspects of the History of Irish Dancing*, Cork, 1994

_____, *Irish Dancing Costumes: Their Origins and Evolution*, Cork, 1996

Dunlevy, M, *Dress in Ireland*, London: Batsford, 1989

Gall, S, 'The Wexford Feis', in *The Catholic Bulletin*, vol II, p 469

Gordon Bowe, N, 'Two Early Twentieth-Century Irish Arts and Crafts Workshops in Context: An Tur Gloire and the Dun Emer Guild and Industries' in *Journal of Design History*, Oxford University Press, 1989, vol 2, pp 194 – 206

Irish Independent, Dublin, 1922, 27 September, p 3, Dublin 1924, 13 August, p 3

Jones, L, 'The Myth of Irish National Costume' in *Ulster Folk and Transport Museum Year Book*, 1971/72, pp 13 – 15

Joyce, P W, *Social History of Ancient Ireland*, London, 1903

Kinney, T and Kinney, M W, *The Dance: Its place in Art and Life*, London, 1914

Larmour, P, *The Arts and Crafts Movement in Ireland*, Belfast: Friar's Bush Press, 1992

Leabhar Na mBan 'A Note on Irish costumes', Dublin, 1919, p 27

Lonergan, P H, 'Irish Dancers in California', in *The Gael*, October 1904, p 331

McClintock, H F, *Old Irish and Highland Dress*, Dundalk; Dundalgan Press, 1950

Mr Punch's Irish Humour in Picture and Story, London: The Educational Book Co Ltd, *c.* 1910

O'Curry, E, *Manners and Customs of the Ancient Irish*, Dublin, 1873

O'Dowd, A, *Common Clothes and Clothing 1860 – 1930*, Dublin: National Museum of Ireland, 1990

O'Kelly, H , 'Reconstructing Irishness: Dress in the Celtic revival 1880 – 1920', in Ash, J and Wilson, E (eds) *Chic Thrills: A Fashion Reader*, London: Pandora Press, 1992

O'Neill, T, *Life and Tradition in Rural Ireland*, London: J M Dent & Co, 1977

Ossorin, 'The Revival of Irish Costume' in *The Gael* September 1903, p 314

Sheehy, J, *The Rediscovery of Ireland's Past: The Celtic Revival 1880 – 1930*, London: Thames and Hudson, 1980

Sutton, E F, *Weaving: The Irish Inheritance*, Gilbert Dalton Ltd, 1980

The Viceregal Garden Party: How to Dress in Irish Materials, Dublin: The Freeman's Journal, 1912 (pamphlet)